How to Save for Retirement And Use Your Savings TODAY

Retirement Planning and Rapid Wealth Creation For the Family

By Dan Chipman

Introduction

Why?

If you ever wondered if it would be possible to plan and save for retirement, while actually improving your current financial condition and allowing you and your family to enjoy more of your life today, I've got good news for you. **Not only is it possible, but it is far easier than you may have imagined it would be!**

Whether you're planning to save for retirement for the first time, whether you have already implemented a plan, or even if you are already retired, your family, including children and grandchildren, can benefit from this information. There is no magic pill for retirement planning, and all plans have their unique circumstances. Make no mistake, saving money is a discipline that has to be learned and is not easy. By picking up and looking into this book, I assume you have some financial discipline or desire to have it.

What this book will do is show you a straight-forward, logical way to save for retirement, while showing you a way to use

that money as though you had never touched it. You will learn how to put together a solid retirement, as well as increase your cash flow in the years leading up to retirement. You will literally get your money working in two different directions at once so that you can live today while saving for tomorrow. Just by picking up this book and implementing the simple strategy outlined, you could easily save between $100,000 to $200,000 over your lifetime if you are currently using credit cards or financing major expenses. You may not be the only one benefitting if you read this book; your children will also greatly benefit if you read this book and implement the plan for them that I describe. So without any more hype, I will go over a few things that may be on your mind, either consciously or subconsciously, before we begin.

Making a Retirement Plan without knowing how is like being dropped off on a deserted island or in a thick rain forest. This book will be your map, tour guide, and compass.

I DO NOT want your money if you feel you're not going to benefit from this book. Hopefully this introduction will let you know whether or not this book is right for you before you even buy it. Be sure to read it through before you buy. The last thing I want to do is sell you something if it is not going to be of any value to you.

The concepts I will explain, including the methodology of creating and implementing a plan, will be straight-forward and easy to follow. This book will reveal some of my knowledge as a previous Financial Advisor and Life Insurance Agent. In the first 4 chapters I will get you to think about what is important to have in your retirement plan, including a simple financial concept that is only understood by the wealthy. This will improve your financial condition significantly in pre-retirement. In the last 6 chapters, I will reveal the ideal investment vehicle for implementing your plan, describe the benefits, and then take you through a checklist to guide you on your planning journey. I am not trying to sell you any specific product other than the information in this book. My goal is to motivate anyone who has ever wanted to start, tweak, or guide others toward a secure retirement. Additionally, I will provide you with a thorough understanding of how your specific plan can monetarily benefit you in the years leading up to retirement. You will not get to the end of this book only to find out that you need to plop down more dollars in order to get the rest of the story. You will get enough information in this book to create a roadmap and initiate a plan. You will have everything you need. You will have to make choices particular to your own plan, but I will attempt to give you a checklist of what is needed and enough information to get you started.

This will not be complicated. The Financial World is very complex and confusing, even to the so-called experts. If I can get you to understand how to save for retirement and how to set up a plan that allows you to enjoy life more before retirement, the actual implementation of the plan will seem trivial. **Even if for some reason you cannot or do not wish to implement the plan, you will gain knowledge in this book that will allow a spouse, child, or grandchild to benefit from what you, the reader of this book, have learned. It will be beneficial to you.**

"$307,750 - median wealth of investors who did financial planning vs. $122,000 for nonplanners, according to Annamaria Lusardi of George Washington University and Olivia Mitchell of Wharton School of Business."

- May 2013 *Money* Magazine

Chapter X

What This Book is Not

I'm sure you have already found quite a few books on Retirement Planning, or How to Save For Retirement. Most are excellent books which provide detailed analysis of many different aspects of Financial Planning. They have given you a base of knowledge in understanding what I would call Traditional Retirement Planning.

Traditional Retirement Planning, in its simplest form and from a financial perspective, consists of knowing where we are today and figuring out where we want to be at some future point. We are in a car going from point A to point Z. We may also want the car to go through points B, C, D, etc. before we end up at Z. To figure out where our point A is, and to figure out all the additional points where we want our car to stop along the way, we need to go through a process to determine this. I will illustrate a Financial Planning Process below.

Procedure to create a Traditional Retirement Plan

1. Figure Out where your point A is. Look at Net Worth: Assets minus Liabilities.

2. Set Goals. Determine Points B, C, D,..Z.

3. Look at your Budget. Understand your revenue (salaries, etc.) minus your expenses.

4. Figure out what it takes, financially, to reach points B, C, D, and Z.

5. Prioritize, or eliminate a point (C, for example) if you cannot financially reach all the points. Or compromise; still try to reach all points, but lower amounts toward each goal.

6. Figure out if your family could still make all destination points if you were not here tomorrow. Figure out if you could still hit all destination points if you or your spouse became disabled.

7. Figure out what is the best strategy to minimize the tax impact so that more of your net money is going towards your goal.

8. Choose tax-advantageous investment products.

9. Figure out what is the best mixture of investments to give you the return you desire based on your tolerance for risk.

10. Implement the plan immediately. Time is money. Set up the plan on automatic deduction from your checking account into your investment account.

11. Update the plan as life changes. Meet regularly with your financial advisor to make sure you are optimizing the plan.

So at this point we have a basic understanding of the process used to build a traditional financial plan. Traditional financial planning is a good thing. It helps us to quantify what is needed to reach our goals. It forces us to prioritize what is important in our lives, and it tells us where and how much of our money should go to that goal. Financial planners have helped many people reach their goals. A sound financial plan can lead you to a much better place than you were before you implemented a plan.

However, this book is not a how-to guide on traditional retirement planning. My goal in this book is to bring value to your retirement planning process and to pull out some aspects of the planning process; I will not be trying to teach Traditional Retirement Planning. I will actually uncover and explain the use of one of the products that has been in existence for many, many years, but has not been explained effectively to the person who is not in the financial services business. **I will be focusing in on guiding you to make a rock solid retirement plan for you and your family, but also want you to be able to enjoy the same money you are putting toward retirement – TODAY, in the present!** I'm sure you're thinking you cannot save for retirement and use that same money today, but I will prove you can actually do just that. **You can get your money literally working in two directions at once!**

Before we begin to look at designing a plan for you and your family, I want to explain why I feel there is a need to look beyond traditional retirement planning. Even with all of the good traditional planning products and methodology in place, people are struggling. People who once thought they had a good plan in place are worried that they will not have enough in retirement. Many are not able to enjoy their current lives today, much less save more toward retirement. If you are like many Americans, you are probably apathetic towards saving for retirement and perhaps bitter that your current planning has not panned out better. There are some things going on in our financial lives of which we may not be aware. Let's see if we can briefly look at what may be causing some of this misunderstanding. I will list a few points of discussion and analyze the validity of each.

Discussion points related to your goal to save:

Risk is in the Markets. Markets have been going up and down for years. No doubt we all witnessed a big drop in the stock market in the 2000's. To many of us, it was the worst we had seen. To some of us who may have expected the markets to generally trend up year after year, it was a real wake-up call. It made many suddenly realize just how much risk they had been taking in the financial markets. One way a good plan mitigates the potential loss is through asset allocation. This is how we spread our assets into different classes. The old adage "don't put all your eggs in one basket" comes to mind. A good investment portfolio compliments asset allocation by systematically rebalancing the portfolio. Rebalancing systematically sells a little out of one asset class that has been performing well and buys into another asset class that has not been performing well. The old adage "Buy Low, Sell high" applies here. This works best in tax-deferred investments as the rebalancing does not trigger taxable capital gains. The bottom line is that even with a well balanced portfolio we could see prolonged periods of losses. Even if we go 15 years with gains, we can never be too confident that what happened in the 2000's may happen in the 2020's or 2030's, perhaps right when we decide to retire.

Social security and Pensions are evaporating. Social security is currently expected to run out of money in 2033. That's approximately 20 years from the published date of this book. Although politicians most likely will not cut current retiree's social security, people who have not yet retired should plan to have much less in social security benefit when they retire. Predicting how much social security will be available for you when you retire may be tricky, but if you are still a ways from retirement, you should not count on social security for retirement. Pensions - money paid out by companies to their employees - are in the same boat. Most companies still allow you to put your own pre-tax money into a 401k, and may even match a portion of your contribution. If you work for the federal, state, or local government and were initially offered a pension, be wary of getting what was promised if you are still a ways from retirement.

Cash Flows are more erratic, and people are making less and spending more. Americans used to work longer in one place and stick with a particular career path. Today, people tend to switch companies or even career paths. They get laid off more frequently. They get divorced more frequently. They have to pay more for food and gas. They are seeing a general trend towards rising taxes. The cash flow, inflowing revenue minus outflowing expenses and taxes, has therefore become more erratic for most families. I'll compare two graphs to illustrate the problem it is causing for the traditional financial plan.

Traditional Retirement Plan
Cash Flow Assumption

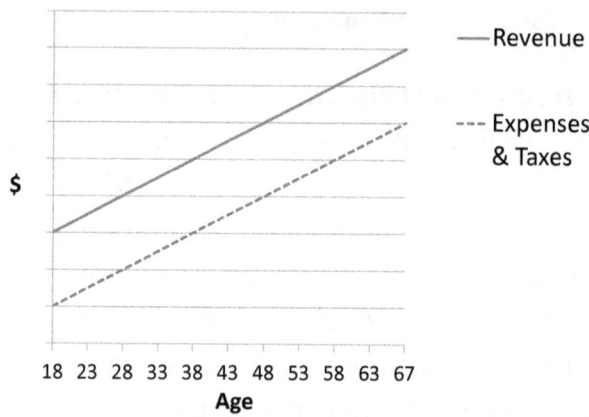

——Revenue

--- Expenses
& Taxes

Real World
Cash Flow

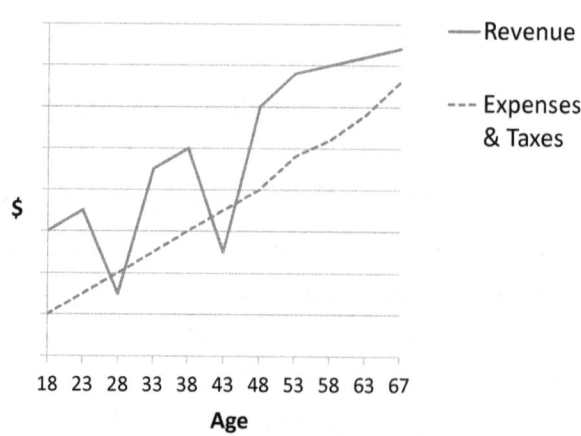

——Revenue

--- Expenses
& Taxes

The two graphs illustrate the fact that at certain times in our lives, our cash flow may go from positive to negative. This may occur multiple times. Many have to cash in on their current retirement savings, which results in less for retirement, not to mention the potential for penalties and fees.

People put money into buckets, but the money is used only once toward their specific need. With most traditional retirement products, money goes into buckets and is ultimately used for the specific need for which they are designed. The money hopefully grows over time, but is used only once years after it was put into the bucket. In my way of looking at it, the money is static, not dynamic, during the years it is set-aside.

Restrictions on the use of investments. As touched on above, there are many restrictions on how we can borrow or take money out of a traditional retirement investment. This gives us much less flexibility during our pre-retirement years to adjust to life's changes or set-backs.

Banks make more money off of us than we realize. If you want to buy a car or go on a really nice vacation, and if you do not have enough cash, you usually take out a loan from a bank. **You buy a car or go on vacation with the use of that money, then you pay the bank for the next 3-5 years. At the end of the 3-5 years, the bank has all of the principle back, plus any interest. Wouldn't it be nice if we could borrow from one of our own investments instead of from the bank and put the principle plus the interest back into our own investment?**

Consider the typical American Family. Approximately 20 % of our disposable income is spent on transportation (automobiles), 30 % is spent on housing, and 40 % is spent on living (clothes, food, vacations, etc.). If we are lucky we save the remaining 10 %. The bank gets our principle plus interest when we finance or lease a car. The bank gets almost half the value of our home in interest. When we take vacations or buy major appliances, we use our credit cards or take out loans. The problem is most all of the items above are typically financed by other banking organizations, not ourselves.

When you add up all the interest that the family is paying out, **it has been estimated that approximately one third (33%) of every disposable dollar is paid out in interest.** So let's see if you were paying attention. You are saving 10% of your disposable income (if you are lucky), but you are paying out 33% of your disposable income in interest. So we have a 3.33 to 1 ratio of interest paid out to savings.

Imagine being in a canoe and trying to paddle against the current. You are paddling hard enough to make the canoe go 1 mph with no current, but the actual current coming from upstream is moving at a rate of 3.3 mph in the opposite direction. You may think you are moving forward if you keep your eyes down and focused at the bottom of the canoe. But when you look up toward the shore, you see that you are moving backward at a rate of 2.3 mph.

Wow, no wonder so many of us are struggling! If you get a random selection of 10 Americans in a room and start talking finances, most all of them will focus on getting a high rate of return on the portion they are saving. Not one is focusing in on the amount of interest they are paying! They say the definition of insanity is "trying the same thing over and over and expecting a different result". I wonder if that definition was derived by looking at the people in that room.

In summary, Americans have been conditioned to think that the bank is where we go when we need any sort of financing. Since we have been conditioned to think that way, we fork over approximately one third of all our money to that end, and continue to have water cooler discussions with our friends about getting better rates of return. Ignorance is bliss!

As mentioned above, this book is not a book on Traditional Retirement Planning. However, when you are done reading this book you will know exactly how to save for retirement and have more money available today! If there's a part of you that doesn't truly believe you can do it or deserve it, then it won't happen. You won't be able to make yourself take action and do what needs to be done to save for retirement.

Taking Action! If you don't take action, you can look out of your window and see a Porsche in your mind all day forever, but one will never show up in your driveway. If you imagine that Porsche every day and do everything possible to get it, you will ultimately own it.

Let's Begin!

"If you don't design your own life plan, chances are you'll fall into someone else's plan. And guess what they have planned for you? Not much."

"Discipline is the bridge between goals and accomplishment."

"Formal education will make you a living; self-education will make you a fortune."

"If you are not willing to risk the unusual, you will have to settle for the ordinary."

- Jim Rohn

Table of Contents

Chapter 1:

Clearing Your Mind of Filters and Setting Goals

I'm going to get you to set your goals down at the end of this chapter. But to do this, I want you to forget what you know about saving money and saving for retirement. What we want to do is change the paradigm and get you to think outside the box.

To do this, let's take a math quiz. When I was in fifth grade, my teacher gave me and roughly 19 other students a math problem that went something like this:

Teacher: "Without lifting your pencil off of the paper, connect the dots below using 4 lines"

• • •

• • •

• • •

   I remember being a little lost trying to solve this puzzle. No matter how many times I tried to connect the dots within the 4 corners, I couldn't do it. What the teacher reminded us later was that a line could go to infinity, and so you could extend the lines outward beyond the 4 corners of the dots. The answer looked like the following:

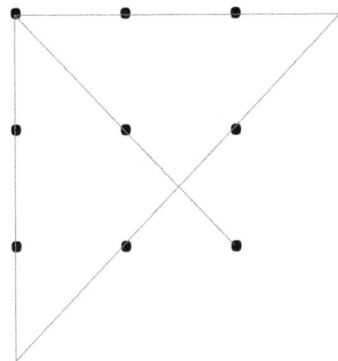

Only 2 out of 20 got the correct answer. The 2 were able to get the problem right by shifting their usual way of thinking. They changed the paradigm.

To save for retirement, we need to change our way of thinking through traditional retirement planning. **Forget everything you have heard about specific retirement products and terms, for it is probably just going to clutter your thinking. We need a fresh new approach.**

Ok, we have decided to put our pre-conceived notions aside. Let's take a deep breath. Get in your favorite yoga position and go to your happy place. Maybe your happy place is something like the scene out of the Corona commercial where you and your spouse are staring at the vast ocean from your beach chairs. Maybe your happy place puts you in a scene like the popular movie Raising Arizona where you and your wife are seated at dinner watching over your many children and grandchildren. Wherever that happy place is, go to it now.

Reflect on what you would like to do with your life if money was not an issue. I know you may be thinking "but money is an issue!". Relax, I will show you how to create more money today and towards retirement, but I want you to get out of your comfort zone a little because your world is getting ready to be a little brighter. List what you want to happen. To make this easier, list the following categories:

Although your goals may vary from the ones I've listed below, let's assume your goals ended up looking something like this:

Goals for you and your family pre-retirement

-    Pay a little extra on our mortgage
-    Pay off existing loan and credit card debt
-    Have a safety net in case of emergencies
-    Get children through a 4 year college
-    Vacation every year to the beach
-    Travel somewhere overseas every 5 years
-    Buy car every 3 years (upgrade 2 cars)

Goals for you and your family post-retirement

-    Have house paid off
-    Increase vacations to twice a year
-    Live comfortably
-    Dabble with a part-time business

Goals for family if you pass away today

-    I want my spouse to live comfortably
-    I want my children to attend college
-    I want to give a little to charity

Now let's jot down some numbers on a spreadsheet that monetarily reflect some of our goals just for illustration purposes. It's ok if you do not know all the estimates at this point, and you will ultimately either figure these out or get the help of a trusted advisor. Please note that inflation can really change a financial picture, so make sure to get some sort of help. If you do a rough calculation, use calculators or web resources that factor in inflation. In Chapter 9, I list some resources to assist with this calculation.

Everything below the first row in the table below is represented in $1,000's of dollars:

Age	45	46	47	48	49	50	51	52	53	54
AMP	2	2	2	2	2	2	2	2	2	2
Vac.	1	1	1	2	2	3	2	2	2	2
Coll.									25	30
Cars				15			20			25
Debt	12									
Sub	15	3	3	19	4	5	24	4	29	59

Total = 165 (1,000's)

In the chart, the following abbreviations were used to simplify the spreadsheet:

AMP = Additional Mortgage Payment
Vac. = Vacations
Coll. = College
Sub = Subtotal

I purposely did not extend this out too far. I used a hypothetical example of a person 45, and extended out the family's projections for 10 years. Obviously, you would want to take this out further to properly plan for all expenses up to and including retirement. I used a 10 year timeframe for this illustration just to show how you would want to quantify your goals. Note that there are a lot of financial costs even in a 10 year period prior to retirement (Again, not even a complete pre-retirement projection here). Also, remember what I stated earlier, that **Americans spend a third of their disposable income on interest**. The above calculation only includes an approximation of the true costs. It does not factor in the interest that most Americans would end up spending (Take $ 165,000 x 3/2 = $ 247,500 actual costs will actually be paid out once you factor in the interest). The average American pays one third of his/her disposable income on interest. They take out loans, finance houses, finance education, max out credit cards; thus digging a hole that is very hard to leave. Think of the average American who finances a car through the bank. They borrow money from the bank, pay the bank back, plus the interest. At the end of 4 years or so, the bank has all the money that was loaned out plus the interest. But let us not get too worried, we will find a better solution; **one that allows you to get back your principle plus the interest you would have paid to the bank**.

We will look at the goals I've listed above, as an example, to illustrate how we can save for retirement while we rapidly build wealth that we can use. At this point we have a positive outlook on our goals, we know a little better what we want out of our life, and we have an open mind about how to do this. Now we need to figure out how to get there.

In the next three chapters we will envision some of the main concepts we would like to be a part of our retirement plan. Chapter 2 focuses on Pre-Retirement, Chapter 3 pertains to Post-

Retirement, and Chapter 4 pertains to Protection of your loved-ones should you pass away or become disabled. Chapter 5 then introduces you with the ideal planning solution to meet all facets of your planning.

Got your seat belt on?

Chapter 2:

Learning How To Have Your Cake and Eat It Too:

Pre-retirement Planning Concept

This is an exciting chapter because it explains how we are going to make our savings work for us in the years leading up to our retirement.

The concept is based on recycling money. I stumbled onto this concept when I was learning how to pay down my mortgage quickly. The concept is simple, and just don't worry for a minute while I digress and give you a mortgage example. If you are making more money than you are spending (and you only apply this concept if that is the case) then you do this: You open up a line of credit, say for $5,000. Then you take out a good portion of the line of credit in month one, about $4,000, and write an additional premium payment on top of your usual mortgage payment. So in month one you have paid $4,000 extra dollars to the principle only, not the interest. You just took about 2 ½ to 3 years off your

27

mortgage, and use the rest of the year to pay down the line of credit. You pay your usual monthly mortgage payment each month while paying down your line of credit. At the end of the year, you have paid off the line of credit, so you are ready to do it all over again. Day one of year 2, you write down another additional mortgage premium payment of $4,000, then use the rest of the year to pay off the line of credit with the bank. In this way you are literally cutting your mortgage in half while recycling your line of credit money over and over again. I realize that this is a unique way to cut into a mortgage since most of what you pay initially is interest; therefore you are paying a little interest for the line of credit, but you are cutting out much more in mortgage interest that you would have been paying over the years. But let's not even worry for a moment about the interest, that is not where I want you to focus. My point is that through this process I learned how to use the same money year after year to cut into the interest on my mortgage. The only problem was that I was using the bank's line of credit each year, so I was paying that money back to them. I kept thinking, "what if I could find a way to pay back myself and recover the principle plus the interest".

Now let's forget I even mentioned a mortgage situation above and focus on a hypothetical investment. Let's look at what could happen if we took an investment, let's not worry about what investment it is (remember what I said about forgetting what we know about investments for the moment), and apply a similar method that I used with mortgages. Let's assume I have an investment of $5,000. If we could take that $5,000 and apply it to something we want to pay off and also pay ourselves back during the year by paying back into the investment, we would end up at the end of the year where we started with our investment and, at the same time, we would have paid off the thing we wanted to pay off. In the next year, we could do the same thing again. After 20 years, we recycled the same $5,000 over and over again to buy $100,000 worth of something!

So let's take a fun real world example. Let's say I want to pay for all my family vacations throughout the year. I estimate that this comes to approximately $5,000 a year. I decide to take $5,000 out of an investment. I get a check in the mail, revenue, that increases my total family income by $5,000, and I pay for all my family vacation needs throughout the year. I book the flights, rent the beach house, or whatever else is required to line up the vacation. Over the next 12 months, I pay myself back into my investment at a rate of $417 a month. At the end of the year, I have $5,000 back in my investment and I have paid for all my vacation needs. The next year I do the same thing. I do this for 20 years. I have used my $5,000 investment to purchase $100,000 worth of vacation needs. At the end of 20 years I still have my original $5,000 investment.

Using the example above, let's compare 2 people, Jack and Sue.

Jack does not recycle his money. Jack spends $5,000 dollars a year to go on vacation. At the end of 20 years he has spent a net $100,000. His financial position has been lowered by $100,000 over 20 years due to these specific circumstances.

Sue recycles her money. Sue spends $5,000 dollars a year to go on vacation. At the beginning of each year she takes $5,000 out of an investment and pays for all her vacation needs. Then she pays at a rate of $417 a month back into her investment. She does this same thing for 20 years. At the end of 20 years she has spent

$100,000, but she also received $100,000 (20 checks times $5,000 each), so she has spent a net 0. Her financial position remains unchanged over 20 years due to these specific circumstances.

Which person's strategy would you rather pursue? I think you would agree with me that you would rather pursue Sue's strategy of recycling money.

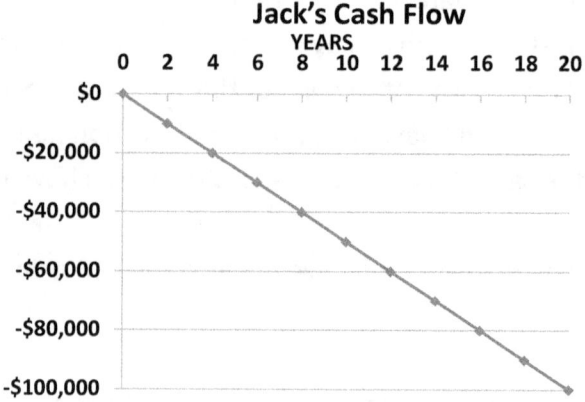

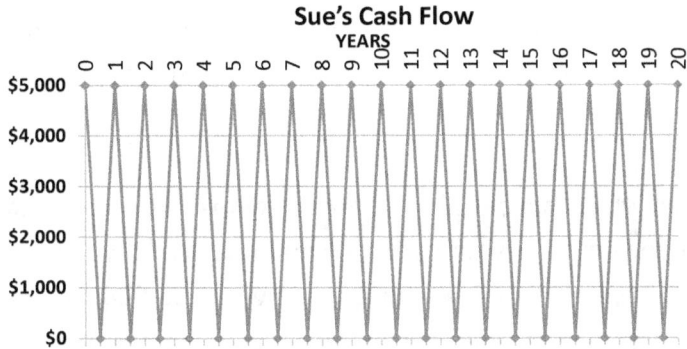

Sue's money rotation follows a cyclical pattern as illustrated below:

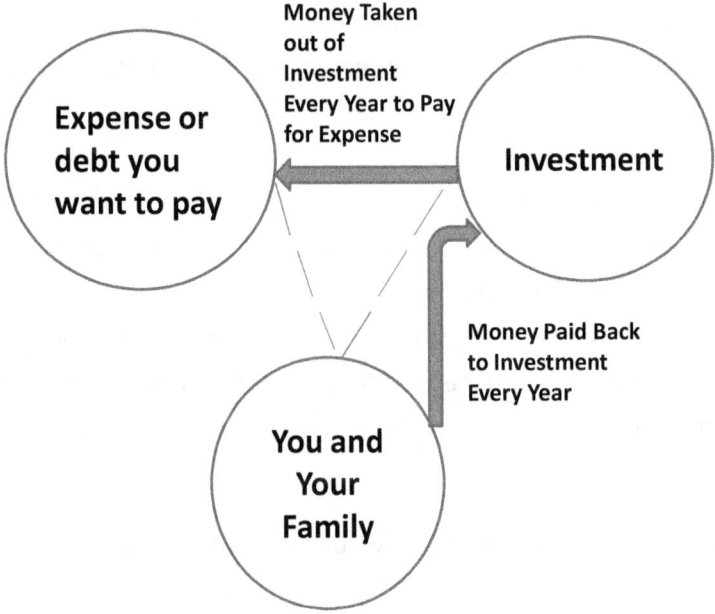

Your investment pays the expense/debt (after passing through your checking account – illustrated in the picture above as a dotted line), and you pay back your investment. At the end of the cycle, preferably after a year, we are starting again with $5,000 in the investment.

Even if what I have explained above seems a little fuzzy, take a different look at it. Is your cash flow not improved if you received a check every year? Imagine yourself receiving a $5,000 check every year for twenty years that you had not previously been receiving. Does that help you understand the benefit of recycling your money? If not, consult your physician!

Compare that to paying cash for something. You paid for something in cash; great, but you could only use that cash once. I propose the method above beats buying anything on credit, financing, or even paying for something in cash. Wild concept I know, but keep thinking about it.

I realize that for most investments, if we take money out of it, it will not continue to grow. I also realize that there is a cost usually associated with taking money out of an investment. I have purposely left those out of the above illustrations so that you could focus on learning the concept of recycling your money, or using the same money over and over again to purchase different things.

Look at the expenses that you subtotaled in the last chapter (Subtotal Amounts are in $1,000's of dollars).

Age	45	46	47	48	49	50	51	52	53	54
Sub	15	3	3	19	4	5	24	4	29	59

Now imagine that you had an investment that you could recycle so that at least some, if not all, of the expenses mentioned above (and in the last chapter) could be paid for each year by the investment. By the following year, all of the money is back in the investment, and you repeat the process.

There is a scene that my daughter and I like in the movie <u>Despicable Me</u> where Gru (played by Steve Carell) says in his Eastern European accent "Light Bulb" (pronounced Light...Bulb!) when the girls that he has adopted have found a way into Vector's Fortress by selling cookies. If you do not have the Light Bulb moment here, it is perfectly ok. Re-read the chapter, look in the mirror, and do your best Steve Carrell "Light Bulb".

Chapter 3:

Creating a Reliable and Predictable Retirement:

Post-Retirement Planning Concept

Do you have an idea of what you want out of your retirement plan?

Do you know what amount of money you need to retire?

Do you want a plan that is reliable?

Do you want a plan that is predictable?

Do you want a plan that steadily goes up in value?

Do you want a plan that does not go down in value?

Do you want a plan that allows you to take money out tax-free or with the lowest possible taxes?

Do you want peace of mind with your retirement plan?

Do you want a plan that does not require you to use dice or crystal balls?

Do you want a plan that is easy to implement?

Do you want a plan that you can make adjustments to as life changes?

If you answered "yes" to most of these questions, then you are reading the right book. Most people who have never planned for retirement would most likely answer, "Of Course". But ask anyone who has been involved with retiring or planning for retirement, and they most likely will look at the questions above and say "there is no such thing". They have been conditioned to traditional retirement planning and traditional retirement products which require a certain amount of risk to achieve a desired reward. Why is it that you do not hear any alternatives? Because the financial industry is making money off of you! They collect 33 % of all your disposable income in interest. I'm not saying that traditional retirement products are necessarily where they get that interest, but remember many of the financial products sold in this country are tied in with banking, loaning, or credit card functions. That is where they make the big money off of you. Given this situation, why would they want you to know anything different?

Let's go briefly through each question, and see if we can decide what we would want our ideal post-retirement plan to look like.

Do you have an idea of what you want out of your retirement plan?

Most people, if they had a choice, would answer "I would like a plan that I know would be there in the future and that I can actually know what amount would be there for me in retirement". So having a plan that is somewhat **risk-adverse, accountable, and predictable** would be a good quality of the plan.

Do you know what amount of money you need to retire?

This is actually a 2-part question. **You want to figure out how much money you want every year to come to you in retirement. Then you need to work backwards to figure out how much total you need on retirement day to last into the full post-retirement period.**

Most retirement planners are now saying that you really need as much money coming in at retirement that you had coming in prior to retirement. I know you may think this sounds like a lot, but the reality is that inflation is projected to go up. So even if you are hoping to have your mortgage paid off by the time you retire, prices are projected to rise enough to cancel this out. If you want to take a look at this yourself, take a look at your current family revenue (salaries, etc) and expenses. If you are currently paying on a mortgage, but can safely predict that you can eliminate it, do that. Also deduct any other expenses that may disappear in post retirement. Then actually add back anything that will be an additional expense such as long term care premiums or additional vacations, etc. You can use a spreadsheet of your own to at least get a ball park estimate of what you need.

Now that you know, or have a ball park idea of this, you back into the amount needed on retirement day. There are also some rule of thumb guides used by planners such as the 4 % rule, etc. It basically says you want to withdraw 4 % of your nest egg into retirement. To find the amount of nest egg, you simply take the amount you want to come to you in one year, and you multiply by 25. For a very simple illustration, let's say your family was making $40,000 a year pre-retirement. You follow the general rule that says you want to keep 40,000 a year coming in post-retirement. Using the 4% rule, you multiply $40,000 X 25 to get $1,000,000. Yep, you need a million dollars in total nest egg to retire and safely withdraw $40,000 a year. We will go through another example in Chapter 6 which illustrates this in a little more detail and will factor in some other things like any pension, 401K, Traditional or Roth IRA money.

Do you want a plan that is reliable?

There is **no actual guarantee on any of the money that is currently in your pension, 401K, Traditional, or Roth IRA.** The world market is in a precarious place and basically unchartered waters as world governments continue to slide further and further into debt. Credit rating agency Standard & Poor's (S&P) downgraded its credit rating of the U.S. Federal Government from AAA (outstanding) to AA+ (excellent) on August 5, 2011.

Do you want a plan that is predictable?

In an ideal plan, you would be able to look out to the year that you actually retire and know, with relative **certainty**, what you will have when you retire.

Do you want a plan that steadily goes up in value?

Have you had enough of the roller coaster ride that you've been on in the last few years? Do you wish you could look at your statement and see **increasing values**?

Do you want a plan that does not go down in value?

How would you like get to within a month of retirement only to wake up one morning to find the stock market has just had one of its worst corrections in history, and your **nest egg has just been cut** by one third.

Do you want a plan that allows you to take money out tax-free or with the lowest possible taxes?

This is going to become a bigger issue as time goes by. Ideally I think you would agree that we would want a plan that we could **take out tax-free loans pre-retirement, and ideally get most of the money we withdraw post-retirement tax-free as well.**

Do you want peace of mind with your retirement plan?

I'm sure you are like most people. You would like to set-up a plan and have it on **auto-pilot**, unless you need to change it.

Do you want a plan that does not require you to use dice or crystal balls?

Viva Las Vegas!! Do visions of casino wheels or fortune tellers kind of scare you?

Do you want a plan that is easy to implement?

Most people who are working hard, raising children, or running a business have little time to learn all about the financial world. You just don't have the time to find the one true solution to your retirement question. **"If I could have someone just show me the way to set-up a rock solid plan, allow me to have more cash flow leading up to retirement, and guide me to some great resources to easily implement a plan, I could actually enjoy my life so much more"!** This book and the information in it will do just that.

Do you want a plan that you can make adjustments to as life changes?

As with any plan, we want it to be **flexible.** Traditional retirement planners take our available savings monies and put them in separate buckets. The buckets are designed toward specific goals (like college, as an example). The problem we often run into when life changes or we switch our goals is that the money we have already put towards a goal can not necessarily be switched to another goal. Penalties or fees or taxes may all be accessed, resulting in a less flexible plan. The ideal plan would not limit us if our goals changed.

Chapter 4:

Creating a Solid Defensive Plan:

Planning for Your Family In Case You Pass Away

Planning for your retirement is a lot like planning to play a sport. Let's say you're the coach of a football team. Imagine spending all of your time putting together a great offensive scheme. You focus solely on this, neglecting to put any effort into working with the defense. Game day comes and your team scores three touchdowns but loses the game because the other team has scored six touchdowns. You lost the game because you forgot to focus any effort on the defense.

The same applies to financial planning. You can have the best offense in the world, but if you don't have a solid defense, you most likely will not have a solid plan. **Planning your defensive**

strategy should be the most immediate strategy since you could pass away today, and your most thought-through offensive plan will not have mattered.

Imagine you are 30 years old and have a spouse and 2 children. You spend several months focusing on where to put money assuming you live well into retirement. You assume you will be making money for a long time, so you put your efforts into saving strategies that optimize your tax situation and rates of return. Then you unexpectedly die or become disabled in a car accident. What do your spouse and children do to reach their goals? Does your wife get to live comfortably for the rest of her life? Do your children get to go to college?

Life insurance is most likely the only choice you have to ensure that your family has choices if you pass away. This becomes the defensive part of your retirement plan. Please note that both you and your spouse should get or acquire life insurance in order to make your plan complete. Even if one spouse is earning most of the family income, the other spouse is most likely doing many important things to keep the family running smoothly. Both spouses should have a defensive plan in place, and a licensed, trusted agent can help you to establish the right amounts based on the goals you want reached in the event the unexpected happens. There are two basic types of life insurance, term and whole life insurance, and we will briefly describe each of these next.

Term life insurance is insurance that covers the policyholder's life for a specific period of time. Say you purchase a $250,000 policy for 20 years. You have covered your family for 20 years in the event that you pass away. When the policy expires after 20 years, you no longer own it. **To use a housing analogy, you are renting a house for twenty years.** At the end of twenty years, your lease is up, and you have no equity in the house. All of the premiums you have paid are gone never to return. If you want more term insurance after 20 years, you will have to apply for a new policy. Life insurance, when applied for, requires you to take a basic medical exam. Your life insurance premiums are based on your age and your health, and are formulated by actuaries of the insurance company. Based on the results of the exam, the insurance company rates you and puts you in classes that determine your health rating. The classes may be broken down into three or four categories such as Premium, Standard, and Substandard. The lower you are rated, the higher your premiums for the amount of coverage you desire. Back to the example above, if you had to reapply for term insurance 20 years after you're initial policy, you are definitely 20 years older and most likely less healthy than you were when you initially applied for the insurance. **If you decide to buy more term insurance later in life, you will pay significantly more in premiums.**

Whole Life Insurance is insurance that covers the policyholder's life for their entire life. Say you purchase a $250,000 policy. **In the housing analogy, you own the house and are putting equity into the house each year you own it.** If you reinvest any dividends, your $250,000 policy coverage will actually grow over the years, and you will also be building cash value (equity) in the policy. **In most policies, you can borrow or even take a good portion out of the cash value at any point in your life.** When your policy is paid up, you completely own the policy just as you would own your house. You can set up Whole Life Policies that are completely paid up at a certain time in your life, but the options vary from one insurance company to another.

I also mentioned disability above as being a potential part of your defensive plan. **Disability insurance is coverage for when you become disabled**. It is meant to at least partially supplement your income should you no longer be able to work. Some people may have disability coverage through their work place of employment, but often times it covers only a portion of your previous income. If you do not have disability coverage through your work, or even if you do have some coverage, you probably want to get the help of an agent to determine if the coverage meets your requirements based on your particular goals.

Now that we know the basics of our defensive plan, we can move forward with finding the right plan for you that can meet as many of your goals as possible. If at this point you are saying to yourself "**it sure would be nice if I could find a product that would combine as many of my defensive and offensive goals as possible to make my life easier!**", then keep reading. In the next chapter I will reveal a product that actually incorporates most of the concepts that we have talked about thus far.

Chapter 5:

Putting It All Together:

The ideal Investment Vehicle to Meet Your Needs

At this point we realize that a retirement plan has to focus on pre-retirement planning, post-retirement planning, and a defensive strategy. We looked at some of our goals, have a basic understanding of our budget, and we created a spreadsheet to quantify expenses we will incur pre and post-retirement. We would like a plan that frees up more cash in our pre-retirement years. We want a plan that will steadily grow regardless of what is going on in the markets. We want to have a plan that is predictable and accountable, but flexible to change. We have an open mind about financial products, and we are still putting aside our pre-conceived notions about financial products. The reason we are doing this will now become clearer.

The product I am about to introduce you to is virtually unknown outside of the financial industry. The product itself has been utilized by the wealthy for over 200 years. However, the product has not been properly explained to most people. It may have been put into a category with other similar products that may yield significantly different results than what we are attempting to accomplish. In a nutshell, the product causes some people to have a negative reaction because they have been totally misinformed about it. Therefore I will attempt to explain the main product and tell you specifically how the product will make our plan work properly.

The product that we want to focus on is **Whole Life Insurance.** Whole life Insurance has been around for over 200 years and has stood the test of time. It is a great place to store money and have it generate dividends, all on a tax-deferred basis. Even if the tax laws change, it is a wonderful place to safely put money and get to it whenever we need it. Yes, you can loan yourself your own money whenever you want to. In a more philosophical sense, economic problems are best solved by people freely contracting with one another and with government limited to enforcing those contracts. The best way to do this is through the concept of dividend paying life insurance. It is not a government idea. It preceded the 1913 income tax law idea by a hundred years. It is private property, and only the people who care about their loved ones participate. This is an ideal group of people to be associated with in business.

There are entire books dedicated to explaining how a whole life policy works. **In Chapter 9, I recommend some books to look at if you want to learn more about how a whole life policy works. I will point you in the right direction to get an agent involved who**

can provide a Free Analysis. He/She can walk you through the process and set up your actual policy. For our purpose, which is to get you what you need to know in order to save for a secure retirement while having more money to use today, we will highlight what you need to know in order to get you a plan that is specific to your needs.

Whole Life Insurance can be the perfect financial vehicle around which we construct our personal finances, if we follow some basic rules. **Think of the Whole Life Insurance Product as a financial engine around which we will construct our finances.** We want a Whole Life Insurance product that comes from one of the **Strongest Life Insurance Groups in the World**. Four groups rate companies and are summarized below.

A.M. Best Ratings

A++ and A+ (Superior) - Assigned to companies that have a superior ability to meet their ongoing obligations to policyholders.

A and A- (Excellent) - Assigned to companies that have an excellent ability to meet their ongoing obligations to policyholders.

B++ and B+ (Very Good) - Assigned to companies that have a good ability to meet their ongoing obligations to policyholders.

Standard & Poor's Ratings

AAA extremely strong

AA very strong

A strong

BBB good

Moody's Ratings

Aaa-exceptional

Aa-excellent

A-good

Baa adequate

<u>Fitch Ratings</u>
AAA-exceptionally-strong
AA-very-strong
A-strong
BBB good

There is also a Comdex composite rating for life insurance companies. The Comdex is not a rating itself, but a composite of all the ratings that a company has received. The Comdex ranks the companies, on a scale of 1 to 100, in relation to other companies that have been rated by the services. Generally, **we want a Life insurance company that is in the upper echelon among all these factors.**

Furthermore, **we want Whole Life Insurance from a mutual company. A mutual insurance company is an insurance company owned entirely by its policyholders.** Any profits earned by a mutual insurance company are rebated to policyholders in the form of dividend distributions or reduced future premiums. In contrast, a stock insurance company is owned by investors who have purchased company stock; any profits generated by a stock insurance company are distributed to the investors without necessarily benefiting the policyholders.

The next thing for consideration is to decide if the company offers non direct recognition or direct recognition policies. The important concern between dividend recognition and policy loans is whether or not a policy loan affects the payments of dividends. **Under Non direct recognition loans, the payment of dividends is not affected by a policy loan**. Under direct recognition, the payment of dividends is slightly lowered by policy loans. Be aware that if you die after a loan has been taken on your policy your benefit is reduced by the amount on the loan. I slightly prefer the non direct recognition policy because I know my dividend rate is unaffected when I take out a policy loan. Do not worry too much about this option at this point. I have one policy that is a non direct recognition policy and one that is a direct recognition policy, and I take loans out on both. I do take loans out of my non direct recognition policy more often knowing my dividends are not affected. The important point for now is that you know there are two slightly different variations. When you fully figure out how a loan may impact your policy, and depending on how you want your policy to be affected by this, then you can decide if a non direct recognition or a direct recognition policy is better for your particular needs. Make sure you ask about the dividend history on policies and the interest rate on loans, as they can vary greatly among the different insurers. **The most important thing is to pick a company that has a strong financial portfolio as you will be building your personal finances around it.**

The final thing to consider is the fact that we want a **dividend paying, or participating, policy**. The companies we want to focus on are the ones that have been paying dividends for many years, even through the 1929 great depression and other significant downturns in our economy. We will end up putting a Level Paid-Up Additions Rider, or LPUAR, on the policy. We need to make sure the type of policy we create has a LPUAR available. **The LPUAR is very important to the type of plan that we create because it greatly accelerates the cash value in the plan.** If you want a little further explanation of the LPUAR, your premium can be broken down into the base premium which goes into the traditional life insurance, and extra premium which goes into LPUAR. LPUAR buys some death benefit, and shifts some of the risk away from the insurance company. Therefore, it allows your cash value to grow quicker. In a simplistic, non-life insurance way of explaining it; it's like when you pay additional premium payment on your mortgage; it goes directly to principle and grows your equity quicker. I realize that these are totally different products but, as far as growing cash value goes, this analogy seems appropriate. **The LPUAR puts your policy into overdrive, allowing it to quickly grow your cash value.**

To understand why a Whole Life Policy is a great way to save for retirement and to use the cash today, let's look at an example of a policy. Do not be overwhelmed by the numbers, I'll try to make it simple. The policy below is for general illustration purposes only, and your individual policy can be significantly different based on your age and health, not to mention your insurable interest (how much insurance you can get). I will look at an example for John Smith, from a non direct recognition policy, which comes from a A+(A.M. Best), AA+(S&P), AA (Fitch), 97 (out of 100) Comdex rated insurance company. I rounded the numbers slightly to make the example a little easier to read. I used projections for John Smith as if he applied for the policy at age 44, and projected them through age 67. **The policy he looked at was for a $100,000 whole life policy. He and his agent added a $50,000 10 year term rider, with a Level Premium Paid-up Additions Rider (LPUAR), and an accelerated benefits rider. The accelerated benefits rider allows him to receive a portion of the proceeds which are otherwise payable on his death if he was suffering from a terminal illness. No additional premium was charged for this rider.**

See the illustration on the next page.

Illustration A – Basic Life Insurance Policy

John Smith
Age 44 Std/Non-Smoker
Initial Annual Premium $2,400
Initial Face Amount $100,000

Amounts in column's 3-8 are in $1,000's

Age	Yr	Pr.	Cum Pr.	Guaranteed		Illustrated	
				CV	DB	CV	DB
45	1	2.4	2.4	0.1	150	0.2	150
46	2	2.4	4.8	0.3	150	0.4	151
47	3	2.4	7.2	1.6	151	2.0	152
48	4	2.4	9.6	3.2	151	3.8	153
49	5	2.4	12.0	4.8	152	5.8	155
50	6	2.4	14.4	6.5	152	8.0	157
51	7	2.4	16.8	8.3	153	10.3	159
52	8	2.4	19.2	10.1	153	12.9	161
53	9	2.4	21.6	12.1	153	15.6	163
54	10	2.4	24.0	14.1	154	18.5	166
55	11	2.3	26.3	16.1	103	21.6	119
56	12	2.3	28.6	18.1	103	24.9	122
57	13	2.3	30.9	20.2	104	28.4	125
58	14	2.3	33.2	22.4	105	32.1	129
59	15	2.3	35.5	24.5	105	36.1	132
60	16	2.3	37.8	26.8	106	40.2	136
61	17	2.3	40.1	29.1	106	44.5	140
62	18	2.3	42.4	31.4	106	49.0	144
63	19	2.3	44.7	33.8	107	53.6	148
64	20	2.3	47.0	36.2	107	58.5	152
65	21	2.3	49.3	38.4	107	63.3	156
66	22	2.3	51.6	40.5	107	68.3	160
67	23	2.3	53.9	42.8	107	73.4	164

In the policy above the columns are broken out as follows:

Age – John Smith applied at age 44. During the first year he turned 45, second year 46, etc.

<u>Yr</u> – Policy Duration in years

<u>Pr.</u> – The amount paid in premiums during the year

<u>Cum Pr.</u> – Cumulative premium reflects all the premiums paid up through the number of years.

<u>CV</u> – Cash Value accumulates value during the policyholder's lifetime. The policyholder can use the cash value as a tax-sheltered investment (the interest and earnings on the policy are not taxable), as a fund from which to borrow, as a means to pay policy premiums later in life, or they can pass it on to their heirs.

<u>DB</u> – The amount that would be paid out upon the policyholder's death to their beneficiaries. If any loans are outstanding, they would be deducted from the death benefit.

In the policy above, John Smith pays $2,400 a year for the first 10 years, and when the term insurance expires after 10 years, he pays $2,300 a year from then on. Note that from years 10 to 11 the death benefit actually drops since our $50,000 term coverage ran out but our whole life insurance has actually grown. Our cumulative premium column shows us the total of all our premiums paid up through any year. Notice that we have our policy then broken out between **guaranteed values and non guaranteed values. The guaranteed values are just that – guaranteed. The illustrated scale reflects values based on historical rates of return for the company.** Although not shown here, note that insurance company's also show a 50 % illustrated scale. Your actual illustrations can be projected with the help of a financial agent.

So going over the policy at this point, note that there is a guarantee on your policy. **Life Insurance Companies are regulated and protected by a state guarantee fund.** How many of your retirement investments have a guarantee? This gives you peace of mind. Please note that on the policy, **cash value and death benefit (on the whole life portion) goes up every year and never goes down as long as you pay your premiums.** Note that when you reach retirement, say at 67, you can make your policy paid up, or stop paying the premiums, and start actually withdrawing from the policy. Note also that this policy is providing you basic insurance coverage. You can pay as little as $2,400 a year to keep the policy growing. However, because of LPUAR, it is quickly growing cash value even for this basic amount. Don't worry if this premium seems high, your situation may be totally different. You may have a lower life insurance amount (say $50,000 policy) that would make your premium lower if you were the same age and in the same health condition, or you could put more in the term portion if you needed to lower premiums. I am just showing you a general illustration in order that you might understand the basics of the policy for now.

Now, let's take this same policy, and add additional premium to it without changing any coverage. In whole life insurance you can take cash out of the policy up to the amount you have put in tax-free. Obviously, it is a great vehicle to store extra cash and let the dividends grow tax-deferred. However, **the IRS sets a limit to the amount of money that can be put into a policy before it becomes a Modified Endowment Contract and becomes taxable. Therefore, working with a financial advisor, he or she will let you know the maximum amount that can go into your policy.** In John Smith's particular policy, the maximum was $6,990 per year.

So again, without changing any Life Insurance coverage amounts, we increased the amount going in (Premium) to $6,990 per year.

Illustration B – Same policy with maximum premium paid

John Smith
Age 44 Std/Non-Smoker
Initial Annual Premium $6,900
Initial Face Amount $100,000

Amounts in column's 3-8 are in $1,000's

Age	Yr	Pr.	Cum Pr.	Guaranteed		Illustrated	
				CV	DB	CV	DB
45	1	6.9	6.9	4.7	168	4.8	169
46	2	6.9	13.8	9.6	186	10.0	188
47	3	6.9	20.7	16.0	203	16.8	206
48	4	6.9	27.6	22.5	220	24.1	225
49	5	6.9	34.5	29.6	235	31.9	243
50	6	6.9	41.4	36.9	250	40.3	262
51	7	6.9	48.3	44.4	265	49.0	280
52	8	6.9	55.2	52.1	279	58.4	298
53	9	6.9	62.1	60.2	293	68.4	317
54	10	6.9	69.0	68.5	306	78.8	335
55	11	6.8	75.8	77.0	269	89.9	304
56	12	6.8	82.6	85.8	282	101.6	323
57	13	6.8	89.4	94.8	293	113.8	341
58	14	6.8	96.2	104.1	305	126.8	360
59	15	6.8	103.0	113.7	316	140.5	380
60	16	6.8	109.8	123.5	326	154.9	399
61	17	6.8	116.6	133.5	337	170.0	418
62	18	6.8	123.4	143.7	347	185.8	447
63	19	6.8	130.2	154.2	357	202.3	477
64	20	6.8	137.0	164.8	367	219.6	497
65	21	6.8	143.8	175.4	375	237.4	518
66	22	6.8	150.6	186.2	384	256.0	538
67	23	6.8	157.4	197.1	393	275.5	559

This is interesting. It shows us that the policy could grow significantly higher and more efficiently with more cash added. To sum up both Illustrations after 23 years see below:

	Cum. Prem.		CV	Guaranteed % Incr.		CV	Illustrated % Incr.
A	53,900		42,800	-21%		73,400	36%
B	157,400		197,100	25%		275,500	75%

In the comparison above, the percentage increase compares the amount I have put in to the policy to my total cash value after 23 years. Do not confuse this with rate of return. The rate of return was approximately 2.5 % on the Illustration A Cash return, and approximately 5 % on Illustration B Cash Return. Keep in mind that the 5 % rate of return on Illustration B is on a tax-deferred investment. If you were in a 33 % tax bracket, and had this money in a taxable investment, you would have to get about a 7.5 % rate of return to equal the tax deferred investment.

The reason I compared these two policies was just to show you that **as we put more premium into a Whole Life Policy, keeping the insurance constant, the more efficient it becomes, and it grows exponentially.** Think of it as a financial engine that gets more efficient over time. This is because your money first goes toward paying the insurance then toward growing the policy. Unfortunately, most people do not look at the Whole Life Policy as a great place to store tax efficient money. Most people are conditioned to think, by the media and certain uninformed financial agents, that we should buy the maximum death benefit for the least amount of money. However, buying your policy that way causes your equity to grow at the lowest possible rate. If we once again change the paradigm, we will be able to create an ideal savings vehicle. **We want to buy whatever death benefit is appropriate and store as much money as we can in this tax-deferred, dividend paying investment.** When we get ready to retire, we can take money out of the policy tax-free up to the point we have put money in. The faster the cash value grows, the quicker we can take loans out on our own policy and get ready cash in order to finance our yearly major purchases.

In the examples above, I focused on showing you some policy examples that were general in nature. I showed that we have a great way to save for retirement since the cash value always goes up as long as we pay our premiums. We have a guarantee specifically on our cash values and death benefit. This guarantee does not come with many other traditional retirement products. We also have an illustration that shows us our cash value and death benefits based on 50 % and 100 % of an illustrated projection scale. We saw through the illustrations above that you can pay your premiums into a Whole Life Insurance Policy from a minimum to a maximum point. The less you put into a Whole Life policy, the less efficient it is. **Conversely, the more premiums you put into the policy the more efficient it is**. Most insurance companies will let you lower or even defer premiums for a certain period of time in case there was a need to do this.

Also note that the above illustration was shown for a middle aged standard male. Can you guess what an insurance policy may look like for a young child who is of average health? The policy only becomes more efficient the younger and healthier you are. If you or your spouse are not healthy, you can look into putting your whole life policy on the healthier spouse, then buy term insurance on the less healthy person. As stated earlier, there are many ways to look at setting up policies for each of your family members. Each family has their unique circumstances. You and a financial agent can look at different ways to best protect and insure your family has a vehicle to get back any money you were previously financing.

Now that we better understand the basics of an ideal investment vehicle for our retirement planning, and we realize that it can help us to meet our pre and post-retirement goals, as well as defensive planning, let's move to the next chapter where we will look at an example to better understand the many benefits of what we have created.

Chapter 6:

Case Study:

How the Plan Benefits You & Your Family

Let's start looking at the ways we can actually use our policies. I am writing this, and am excited to do so, because I wish someone had shown me how to efficiently use my policies in my younger days when I was beginning to learn about Whole Life Policies. I would generally go through about as much as we have done up to this point. However, I would always be saying to myself, **"OK, I am putting a big chunk of change into this thing, getting a nice cash value, but not really being coached on how to use the policy"**. So my intention in the remaining chapters is to pick up where most planners stop, and explain **"What's in it for me TODAY?"**

Let's look at 4 people who make up the Smith Family. They are:

John Smith – John works as an engineer at a local Industrial Plant. He makes $50,000 per year. He is 44 years old and in good health.

Mary Smith - works part-time at the local library and makes $20,000 per year. She is 43 years old and in good health.

Amy Smith – Amy is the Smith's daughter. She is 9 years old and in the 3rd Grade. She is in good health.

Jack Smith - Jack is the Smith's son. He is 7 years old and in the 1st Grade. He is in good health.

John and Mary have the following budget:

After tax revenue: $57,000/yr
Expenses: $48,000/yr

John and Mary both take out about 8 % of their pre-tax income and put it toward their respective 401K plans at work. At this point in their lives, they have accumulated the following assets:

John 401K	$100,000
Mary 401K	$75,000
John Trad. IRA	$50,000
Mary Trad. IRA	$25,000
529 for Amy	$15,000
529 for Jack	$10,000
Savings	$5,000

John and Mary have owned their home for 5 years and have 25 more years to pay on their 30 year mortgage.

John and Mary have done some of their own research, and are planning to talk to a financial planner soon to figure out if they are on track for their retirement planning. They believe that if they pay some extra money toward their house payments over the next 15-20 years, they will have their mortgage paid off in retirement. Since the mortgage will be paid off in retirement and the kids are finally out of the nest, they think they can live well having $50,000 per year come to them in retirement. So based on that, and the 4% rule, they estimate they need approximately $50,000 x 25 = $ 1,250,000 in retirement.

Mary likes to read, and before going in to see a financial planner, she sees this book and decides to look into it. She is a little nervous about the markets, and she is worried about saving for retirement. On top of this, she knows they have a lot of car and house upgrades, vacation plans, debts to pay off, not to mention putting Amy and Jack through college. They need to do most of this before they can think of retiring. They decide to go through the advice in Chapter 1 and they write down their goals and quantify them. For simplicity, we will pretend that the expenses listed in Chapter 1 were John and Mary's expenses. As a reminder, we just listed 10 years worth of their expenses to make it easier to follow. John wrote the expenses as the following (subtotal amounts are in $1,000's):

Age	45	46	47	48	49	50	51	52	53	54
Sub	15	3	3	19	4	5	24	4	29	59

With a rough handle on their expenses, they read through the Chapter 9 Resources chapter in the back of this book and they met with a financial planner. The planner ran an illustration for each family member. The policy for John and Mary was shown with the minimum and maximum amount of premium they could put in for the amount of Life Insurance coverage they required. They also had policy's run for each of their children. Mary was the policyholder for Amy, and John was the policyholder for Jack. That way, John and Mary could be the owner of the children's policies until each of their children got out of college and were earning their own income. At that point, they would transfer ownership over to the children.

The policy for John was illustrated earlier in Chapter 5. Mary had a similar policy and is shown with maximum premiums paid. Each child had their own policies, and one policy (for simplicity, only one policy was shown since both of the children's policies looked similar) is shown below. All illustrations are general in nature, and are specific to each individual's age and health. Your particular policies may be different based on your particular circumstances.

See the illustration on the next page.

John's policy with maximum premiums

John Smith
Age 44 Std/Non-Smoker
Initial Annual Premium $6,900
Initial Face Amount $100,000

Amounts in column's 3-8 are in $1,000's

Age	Yr	Pr.	Cum Pr.	Guaranteed		Illustrated	
				CV	DB	CV	DB
45	1	6.9	6.9	4.7	168	4.8	169
46	2	6.9	13.8	9.6	186	10.0	188
47	3	6.9	20.7	16.0	203	16.8	206
48	4	6.9	27.6	22.5	220	24.1	225
49	5	6.9	34.5	29.6	235	31.9	243
50	6	6.9	41.4	36.9	250	40.3	262
51	7	6.9	48.3	44.4	265	49.0	280
52	8	6.9	55.2	52.1	279	58.4	298
53	9	6.9	62.1	60.2	293	68.4	317
54	10	6.9	69.0	68.5	306	78.8	335
55	11	6.8	75.8	77.0	269	89.9	304
56	12	6.8	82.6	85.8	282	101.6	323
57	13	6.8	89.4	94.8	293	113.8	341
58	14	6.8	96.2	104.1	305	126.8	360
59	15	6.8	103.0	113.7	316	140.5	380
60	16	6.8	109.8	123.5	326	154.9	399
61	17	6.8	116.6	133.5	337	170.0	418
62	18	6.8	123.4	143.7	347	185.8	447
63	19	6.8	130.2	154.2	357	202.3	477
64	20	6.8	137.0	164.8	367	219.6	497
65	21	6.8	143.8	175.4	375	237.4	518
66	22	6.8	150.6	186.2	384	256.0	538
67	23	6.8	157.4	197.1	393	275.5	559

Mary had an illustration run with a $75,000 Whole Life Policy with a $25,000 10 year term rider, and LPUAR and accelerated benefits rider just like John's Policy.

Mary's policy with maximum premiums

Mary Smith

Age 43 Std/Non-Smoker

Initial Annual Premium $4,000

Initial Face Amount $75,000

Amounts in column's 3-8 are in $1,000's

Age	Yr	Pr.	Cum Pr.	Guaranteed		Illustrated	
				CV	DB	CV	DB
44	1	4.0	4.0	2.8	104	2.9	105
45	2	4.0	8.0	5.6	108	5.8	109
46	3	4.0	12.0	9.3	111	9.8	117
47	4	4.0	16.0	13.0	116	14.0	128
48	5	4.0	20.0	17.1	122	18.5	140
49	6	4.0	24.0	21.4	130	23.3	152
50	7	4.0	28.0	25.7	141	28.4	169
51	8	4.0	32.0	30.2	153	33.9	184
52	9	4.0	36.0	35.0	165	45.7	195
53	10	4.0	40.0	39.8	176	58.9	207
54	11	3.9	43.9	44.6	154	66.0	185
55	12	3.9	47.9	49.8	170	73.6	197
56	13	3.9	51.9	55.0	180	81.5	211
57	14	3.9	55.8	60.4	191	89.8	223
58	15	3.9	59.8	66.0	202	98.6	232
59	16	3.9	63.7	71.7	213	107.8	243
60	17	3.9	67.7	77.5	224	117.4	254
61	18	3.9	71.6	83.5	235	127.4	265
62	19	3.9	75.6	89.5	245	137.8	277
63	20	3.9	79.5	95.6	256	148.6	290
64	21	3.9	83.5	101.8	266	159.9	304
65	22	3.9	87.4	108.0	276	170.0	317
66	23	3.9	91.4	114.4	286	181.5	331
67	24	3.9	95.3	120.0	296	193.0	346

As mentioned earlier, John and Mary took out policies on each of their children. The children each had their own policy, but for the sake of simplicity, I just show Amy's policy below since Jack's would be fairly similar. Values are shown for every 5 years to simplify the illustration.

Amy Smith

Age 9 Standard

Initial Annual Premium $600

Initial Face Amount $54,750

Amounts in column's 3-8 are in $1,000's

				Guaranteed		Illustrated	
			Cum				
Age	Yr	Pr.	Pr.	CV	DB	CV	DB
10	1	0.6	0.6	0.3	59	0.3	59
15	6	0.6	3.6	2.0	79	2.1	80
20	11	0.6	6.6	4.6	95	5.0	99
25	16	0.6	9.6	7.9	109	8.8	116
30	21	0.6	12.6	12.0	120	13.6	132
35	26	0.6	15.6	17.0	128	19.7	146
40	31	0.6	18.6	22.7	136	27.4	160
45	36	0.6	21.6	29.8	142	37.2	174
50	41	0.6	24.6	38.1	147	49.3	187
55	46	0.6	27.6	47.5	151	64.0	200
60	51	0.6	30.6	58.0	155	81.0	214
65	56	0.6	33.6	69.6	158	103.0	230

John and Mary set up policies for the children so that they could slowly teach their children how to set-up their own financial system. They were looking forward to the days when they could see their children grow financially independent. **Both children's policies were set-up with a guaranteed purchase option which allows them to increase the amount of insurance at certain points in their lives if they so desire.** As mentioned above, John and Mary would retain control of the policies until the children got out of their college years, and then they would transfer the policies over to their children. **The parents would be able to benefit from the policies by taking out loans as needed from the children's policies for college or other expenses.** The children would benefit once the policies were switched into their names, and they could start taking their own loans from them.

When John and Mary got home, they were excited. They believed that they could save for retirement and also pay for more things today by using The Whole Life Policy's just illustrated. To determine if they had enough assets for retirement, they looked at their assets along with the policies that were illustrated for them. At retirement, they would have the following:

	Today	Retirement
John 401K	$100,000	$308,000
Mary 401K	$75,000	$242,000
John Trad. IRA	$50,000	$154,000
Mary Trad. IRA	$25,000	$81,000
John LI Policy		$275,500
Mary LI Policy		$193,000
Total	$250,000	$1,253,500

The amount above assumes a 5 % rate of return on their current IRA investments and used the illustrated scale from the Whole Life policies. With the help of a financial agent, they were able to come up with policies for each of them that would adequately insure them, and allow them to reach their retirement goals.

What really sold the Smith's on the policies was the ability to tap into the same money that they were putting towards retirement as if they had never touched it at all. They could take loans out on any of their family policies throughout their lives, pay off their major expenses with the loan money, then slowly pay back the loan to their own insurance policy. **This is exactly the recycling of money concept illustrated in Chapter Two. It's as if their money was working in 2 directions at once, in fact it was!** The plan was funding their retirement while simultaneously helping them with their short term goals. They found that by following the rules mentioned in Chapter 5, they were able to get illustrations that revealed how they could save for retirement, and also help to pay for much of their expenses leading up to retirement. They fully bought into the idea of using their own policies as a means to finance their expenses. They knew they would be paying themselves back instead of putting expenses on credit cards or borrowing from a bank.

Let's look at how you can use your cash values. You can take loans out of your policy up to about the full cash value (may vary slightly depending on Insurance Company). When you take out a loan, you call an 800 # at your life insurance company or go online and take out a loan with about 2 clicks of the mouse. It is worth noting that when you call and ask for a loan, no one questions what you are using the money for. **Let me repeat, no one questions you about what you need the money for.** It is your money, so this makes sense! Just call your life insurance company and tell them you want a loan. Tell them how much you will pay back every month. The loan can be paid back in 6 months, 1 year, 2 years, you decide.

You may decide to leave your cash value alone and tap into the cash value only as you need it. However, **the more frequently you take loans on your policy, the more that it will help your short term needs and strengthen your cash position. By taking a loan on your policy, you are getting out in front of your money, instead of putting things on credit cards or taking out loans.** It is wise to take loans out on your policies. Keep an eye on your budget so you can pay back the loan. The shorter you make your loan payment term, the quicker you will pay back yourself so that you can take out the next loan for a different reason. Just keep in mind that the shorter the payback horizon, the bigger the monthly loan payment will be.

You can use the loan money for anything. You can use it in an **emergency.** You can use it for a **medical expense.** You can use it for **disability.** You can use it if you **lose your job.** You can even **skip** some of the loan repayments, offering you flexibility. You can use it to pay for **college expenses.** You can use it to pay for **cars**. You can use it to pay for **vacations.** You can use it to pay **extra on your mortgage.** You can use your loan to reduce or **eliminate debt**. You can use it on **business expenses**, including vehicles or equipment. Basically, the sky is the limit, and you are in control because it's your money that you are borrowing.

You can now become your own source of any type of financing. You can have capital whenever you need it. Think of it, you will not have to rely on your employer, the government, or the bank for your financial security. **If you had financed through your local bank 5 cars for $25,000 each and 5 vacations for $5,000 each in your lifetime, that would be $150,000 you paid the bank plus the interest. Wouldn't you rather have all of that money go toward your retirement?**

Under current tax laws, you **can take a loan out of your policy tax-free.** It is not reported as income. When you retire, **you can take money out of the policy tax-free up to the amount you put in.** Then you can borrow on it again or take out more and pay tax. **The loan itself is like a zero interest loan.** Let's say you pay 5 % in interest when you take out the loan, but your cash value grows by 5 % as if you had never touched the policy. So the resulting interest is zero. **When you take income from your policy in retirement, your income is not counted for alternative minimum tax (amt) and will not lower the social security you get.**

Now that we have quickly gone over many of the incredible benefits of a Whole Life Policy, let's look back at John and Mary's situation. When John got home from seeing the financial planner, he put together the spreadsheet below:

Age	Yr	John CV	Mary CV	Exp	Cum. Exp	Total Loans	Cum. Exp After Loan
45	1	4.8	2.8	15.5	15.5	7.0	8.5
46	2	10.0	5.8	3.5	19.0	14.0	-2.0
47	3	16.8	9.8	3.5	22.5		1.5
48	4	24.1	14.0	18.5	41.0	26.5	-6.5
49	5	31.9	18.5	3.5	44.5		-3.0
50	6	40.3	23.3	5.0	49.5	30.0	-28.0
51	7	49.0	28.4	24.0	73.5		-4.0
52	8	58.4	33.9	4.0	77.5	40.0	-40.0
53	9	68.4	45.7	29.0	106.5		-11.0
54	10	78.8	58.9	59.0	165.5	48.0	0.0

He listed the cash values for himself and his wife. Then he listed the expenses that he had put down for the next 10 years. He then added up the cumulative expenses (adding each year's expenses to the total of all the previous years). Next he looked back at the cash values, and figured out how he and his wife could take out loans from their policies over the next 10 years. He assumed that they could pay back the year one loans in one year. The loans from years 2 – 10 would have to be paid back over 2 year periods since they were larger loans. Note that by looking 10 years into the future, he could anticipate when his major expenses would hit, so he could actually get more money out from his policies before the expenses were realized. That way, he and his wife were staying in front of their money instead of having to put anything on loan or credit card. The whole time that they were recycling their money, they were putting money back into their own financial system, and they were avoiding paying anything to the bank.

In the previous example, note that we did not apply any of the money saved in Amy or Jack's 529 plan. If John had used money in Amy's 529 plan, which would have grown from her current $15,000 amount to hopefully more like $25,000, he could use this money to lower some of the college expenses that were in years 9 and 10. Thus he would not have to take out as big a loan in those years as what was shown in the illustration. He would probably want to use the 529 plan money first when Amy went to college since there are potential fees and penalties if he did not use the 529 money for college.

John and Mary were now starting to understand the power of properly using their whole life policies to pay for the bigger expenses in their lives. By understanding that they could have more cash today and pay themselves back, their financial future was looking much brighter. They then set up a meeting with their financial planner to discuss ways to fund their whole life policies. They had always been financially disciplined, and they realized that they would need to continue to do so in the future. In the next chapter, we look at ways to fund their plans.

Chapter 7:

Funding Sources

Funding your plan is not hard or complicated, but it does require you to take initial steps and discipline in order to get it funded. The goal is to re-direct current funding that may be going to other sources, so that your current cash flow is not squeezed. Even if you are currently in debt, or feel you are not making more than you are spending, you can quickly be on the road to financial security. Keep in mind that we are still changing the paradigm, and your mind may be saying "but I have always heard that you should do this instead". Speaking from experience I had the same initial reaction, but once I understood that my money could be working much harder for me, it all started to make sense.

There are many ways to adjust your current cash flow to fund plans for your family. I will list a few of the more popular ways to fund your plan, but ultimately you and your advisor can decide what works best for you.

Use your existing Life Insurance Policies. If you currently have a whole life policy and it is working fine for you, and you are able to take out loans and it is growing nicely, then don't touch your current policy. You might possibly be able to make the loans and all the other strategies in this book work for you to create a better today and a solid future. However, if your policy will not work functionally for you to accomplish the strategies I have outlined thus far, then you have two choices. You can convert or use your existing policy. You can convert your policy to a new, more suitable policy with the help of an advisor. In this case, you could transfer the cash value from the old policy to the new policy as a tax-free exchange. This may dramatically jump start your new policy, and grow the cash value significantly, and most likely would give you a much better policy over the longer term. The other choice would be to use your existing policy, but use the cash value in that policy to pay for all of the premiums in the new policy. Thus you would use your recycling strategy year after year. You would take out policy loans on the old policy to pay for the premiums on the new policy. Make sure your existing policy allows you to take loans from it, and also find out how much interest would be charged to do this.

Reduce the funding going in to your 401K and other retirement plans. Remembering back to John and Mary, they were each putting 8 % of their pre-tax money into their 401K's. Once they looked into each of their own 401K plans, both of their companies were only matching the first 3 % of their money. It is wise to continue to put in what the employer will match since this is an automatic doubling of your money. However, the additional 5 % that they were previously putting in was not being matched. Therefore, they reduced each of their 401K plan contributions from 8 % to 3 % of their pre-tax salary. Also, if they had been putting any money into their traditional IRA's or 529 plan, they would now stop doing this. Again, keep reminding yourself that your new plan will provide flexibility, guarantees, and tax advantages that your traditional government sponsored 401K plan, IRA, or pension plan does not provide.

You can take money out of your IRA or 401K plan. You will want to talk to an advisor and possibly a tax professional before taking money out of your current retirement plan as there could be tax consequences or penalties if you do it incorrectly. If you pulled money out of a Roth IRA, you wouldn't have to pay a tax, but if you were younger than 59 ½, then you may still pay a penalty. You can use a 72 (t) to pull money out of a traditional retirement plan to fund a new plan. The 72 (t) is a method by which you can access your IRA funds prior to age 59 ½. In order to take advantage of this rule, you determine the amount of the annual distribution from your IRA (this is done in a specifically prescribed manner) and then begin taking the distributions. Once you start the 72 (t), you have to keep it going for the longer of five years or until you reach age 59 ½.

Use your bank savings. Money you currently have in a bank or financial institution's money market account is probably getting a small rate of return. Most likely it is being taxed. Now that you understand that you can get your money any time you need it, get that money working harder in your own plan.

Liquidate a portion of any taxable Mutual Funds. Your mutual funds are most likely in fairly risky investments that are left to the whims of the financial market. As you get older, you want a higher percentage of your investments in safer havens. A financial agent can help you to decide how much to liquidate depending on your overall goals.

Temporarily reduce the amount you are paying off in debt. With the help of an advisor, you could tweak your debt structure to possibly free up more cash. This may involve temporarily paying off less in credit card or loan debt. You may only pay the minimums for a while so you can use the freed up cash to start your plan and quickly build cash value. If you were going to refinance your mortgage or credit card debt anyway, then there may be a way to free up some more cash. This will allow you to build cash value so you can start taking out loans on your personal life policies and pay yourself back. If you pay premiums on your policies on an annual basis, you will build up cash value quicker, which will enable you to take a loan quicker and pay off your debt faster. There are many ways to move money around to free up cash and eliminate debt faster, but please seek some professional help on this.

Use bonus or raise opportunities. If you have a raise or bonus coming up, you could put this money towards your plan. You would not likely miss the money since you were not used to having it in the past, and it would be going toward the goal of generating more money for you.

Use your Tax Refund. The definition of a tax refund is a return of your own money for which the government got a tax free loan and you got a zero rate of return. If instead of getting a big refund every year, you adjust your withholding so that the government gets a little less and you get a little more, then you have freed up cash for your plan.

Temporarily Suspend your additional Mortgage Payments. If you are putting extra money into your home equity, think about suspending these payments for a while. The problem with home equity is that you cannot use it once it goes into your mortgage. It is not recyclable like the money you will be putting into your plan. If you lose your job you can tap into the money in your plan but you cannot get to the money in your home. You could take out a home equity loan, but you probably would not be able to re-finance if you had to or qualify for a loan. Your money is locked into your house, and we have all seen that home prices do not necessarily always go up. Once you get your plan funded, and if you want to get your house paid off sooner, you can start to use some of the money from loans to go toward your additional principle payments.

Analyze your lifestyle. Critically look at your current spending habits to see if you can eliminate or reduce some cost. I am probably as bad as anyone at actually trying to make this work, but with willpower, you can achieve some significant savings. Think of it as substituting the minor things so you can achieve bigger goals in your life. Cut the daily stops to the coffee shop. Eat out twice a month, not four times. Cut out cigarettes or bad habits. Wait an extra year to get the car upgraded, and then upgrade it even better. Use coupons if you don't already. Buy presents in the off-season when the prices are down. Buy generic drugs. Carpool to work. Try to plan more and act impulsively less. Wait to watch that movie until it comes out on Red Box or Netflix. Lose the gym membership for half a year when the weather is warm and it is probably healthier for you to be exercising outside. Get hand-me-downs for the children; you can save a ton on this alone. Bypass the snack machine at work and bring fruits and vegetables from your local grocery store. Use pay-as-you-go phones instead of high-priced phones with annual contracts. Use grant money to pay for a portion of college education. I could probably go on for a while, but you get the point. Just force yourself to take a good look at your current spending, and eliminate the things that you can do without. Stay focused on the main reason you are doing this so that you keep your motivation. Keep thinking of that Porsche you want in your driveway and do the little things to own it!

Chapter 8:

Checklist: Setting Up

and Implementing the Plan

We have covered a lot of information in a short amount of time. It is my assumption that by picking up this book and reading it you had certain questions that needed quick answers about how to save for future retirement and how to use your savings today. I hope you feel comfortable by now with your pre and post-retirement goals, and your defensive strategy as well. Now that you understand the methodology behind your savings plan with an emphasis towards rapid wealth creation, I want to include a checklist for you so that you can implement your plan as soon as possible. This checklist is presented below:

Retirement Planning and Rapid Wealth Creation Checklist:

✓ **Ignore all pre-conceived notions concerning traditional retirement planning products.** Keep your inner compass pointed in the direction you want to go. You will hear people come out of the woodwork and tell you why they think investing in a whole life policy is a bad idea. Many times they are not even talking about the same product.

"The dumbest people I know are the people who know it all".

- Malcolm Forbes

✓ **Create a list of Goals**
- Pre-Retirement Goals
- Post-Retirement Goals
- Goals for family if you pass away

You want to list major goals that would not easily be covered in your normal monthly budgeting.

✓ **Quantify the goals you listed above.** Get the help of an advisor, or create a simple spreadsheet like the one illustrated in Chapter 1. You will most likely want to extend it out as far as you feel comfortable with the projections. For simplicity, I chose to only focus for ten years, but you can go out much further if you are comfortable with it. You can build inflation into your spreadsheet. **I'll list a few resources in Chapter 9 to assist with this, including where to go to find an advisor.**

At this point, we could march in to any of our various traditional retirement planners, tell them our goals and budget, tell them our plan for a defensive strategy, tell them our risk tolerance, and let them divide our goals into buckets. Then we could figure out which bucket gets a bigger share of the bucket pie, and we could cap that off with some term or even whole life insurance.

But now that we have read this book, we are more savvy about another way to get all of these goals accomplished without playing the bucket game. We realize that many times in life things happen where we may suddenly lose a job or have an emergency and we may suddenly need cash. We can have a tax-deferred retirement plan with guarantees and flexibility; we can fund it by diverting some of our money that is going into other plans or toward interest payments. We can take out loans on the policy without having any impact on the growth of our cash values (with non direct recognition policies), the net being a zero interest loan. The loan increases the money coming in to our family's cash flow, and can be used to pay towards life's bigger expenses. Then you pay YOURSELF back. You repeat the loan process as much as possible leading up to retirement (and possibly later in life as well) as your budget allows you to do. By doing all of this, you get ahead of your money pre-retirement, and you have created a rock solid post retirement plan, not to mention a solid defensive strategy. The checklist below will steer you in the right direction to make sure you create the right type of whole life policy.

✓ **Make sure you choose a solid financial company.** You want a company that has great A.M. Best, Standard and Poor's, Moody's, and Fitch's ratings. You also want to have a company that has a great Comdex Score.

✓ **Find a mutual company.** A mutual insurance company is an insurance company owned entirely by its policyholders. Any profits earned by a mutual insurance company are rebated to policyholders in the form of dividend distributions or reduced future premiums. In contrast, a stock insurance company is owned by investors who have purchased company stock; any profits generated by a stock insurance company are distributed to the investors without necessarily benefiting the policyholders.

✓ **Pick a company that offers Non direct recognition loans.** Under Non direct recognition loans the payment of dividends is not effected by a policy loan. Under direct recognition, the payment of dividends is slightly lowered by policy loans. Be aware that if you die after a loan has been taken on your policy your benefit is reduced by the amount on the loan.

✓ **Get a dividend paying, or participating policy.** The companies we want to focus on are the ones that have been paying dividends for many years, through the great depression and other significant downturns in our economy.

✓ **We need to make sure the type of policy we create has a LPUAR available.** The Level Paid Up Additions Rider (LPUAR) is very important to the type of plan that we create because it greatly accelerates the cash value in the plan.

In the Chapter 9 Resources section of this book, I will give you some places to look to find an agent. He or she should represent a company that can create the type of policy you are looking for. You will have to choose a company based on your personal experience, or your criteria depending on what is most important to you. Next, you need to set-up an appointment with a financial agent. **I list out resources in Chapter 9 where you can get a free analysis for your situation.** Answer the agent's initial questions so he/she can get to know you and understand your goals and current budget/lifestyle, etc. Explain to the agent that you would like to see illustrations for each of your family members based on their insurable interest (the amount of life insurance appropriate for each family member). Make sure at this point you have a strong mutual company, preferably a non direct recognition company, participating (good dividends) and definitely has a level paid up additions rider (LPUAR). For your children, make sure you get a guaranteed purchase option for more coverage options later in life. Remember that you may want to over fund your policy to build up cash value quicker. Be aware that the agent makes more money the more life insurance he/she sells you. Knowing this, try to find a policy that is adequate for your life insurance needs, but be careful on getting sold too much insurance. You want a policy that covers all your insurance needs if you died today, but you don't want to be worth more dead than alive (just kidding). So once you and your agent have decided on an adequate amount of insurance (say it's a $200,000 policy for you, $100,000 for your wife, and $50,000 for each of your children), let the agent run some illustrations. Back to the checklist:

✓ **Pick a Life Insurance company based on the criteria mentioned above. Set up an appointment with an agent. After answering questions for the advisor, get him/her to run whole life illustrations for all members of the family.** Have the agent run the illustrations with LPUAR included for basic policies. Get him/her to run each policy at the maximum funding level as well. Children's policies may only have one option (basic policy), but make sure you add a guaranteed purchase option rider to get more coverage at later points in their lives.

✓ At this point you have some basic policies to look at; however, the life insurance policies will be contingent on your age and health. With the help of the agent, **you will need to fill out medical evaluations for each family member.** Most likely you will take this home to fill out, and the agent can help both spouses to set up medical appointments. The children usually do not have to take an exam, but the parents have to fill out the medical history of the child. Do not worry, the medical exam is quick and painless. Usually your medical exam can be done in the privacy of your home or office unless the insurance company requires additional tests. You will be asked your medical history, your family's medical history, information about how to contact your primary doctor, lifestyle habits such as smoking, drinking, recreational drug use and exercise, and how much life insurance you are interested in purchasing. Procedures include measurement of your weight and height, Measurement of your blood pressure and pulse, Blood work (to check things such as cholesterol, glucose, protein, and HIV), and Urinalysis (to check things such as protein, glucose, creatinine and cocaine). Note that depending on how much life insurance you apply for, you may only have to go through some of the above. The people that show up at your house or in your office can usually be in and out within 20 minutes, so do not let this process scare you. It is time well spent when you are greatly improving your family's financial future. To quote Nike "just do it".

✓ Underwriting usually takes about a month or less at the better companies. **Then you go back in to your agent and he/she goes over the results with you.** The Life Insurance Company will classify your age and health into categories such as Premium, Standard, and Sub-standard. The lower the classification, the more you will have to pay in premiums. At this point, if your category rating is at the same level that the agent initially ran your illustration, the premiums will stay the same. If you are put into a lower category, you would have to pay more in premiums to get the same amount of coverage that was initially illustrated.

At this point, you will have to decide whether to pay a higher premium to keep the same amount of coverage, or you can lower the insurance to lower the premium. **Once you and your agent decide what is the right amount of insurance for each family member, make sure the agent runs an illustration for basic coverage and maximum coverage (with the LPUAR rider added on both).** You can also ask your agent to run one illustration somewhere in the middle if you are weighing cost versus benefit. Remember that you will be taking loans out of some of these policies, so factor this into your budget. Never forget that you will be receiving revenue when you take a loan, but then you will be paying yourself back on your own schedule and with no interest!

✓ Once you have decided on the right policies, you should receive them within a few weeks after underwriting. You can feel good knowing that if you died today, your family has been fully protected. You can also plan out your first year's payment plans to optimize your cash value growth within your budgeted levels. **Now you can also start targeting which of your major purchase goals, that you had on your goals list, you want to pay for first with your first loan.**

At this point, we have completed our checklist to get you started on your own financial plan. One question you may ask, and it is a fair one, is how soon you can take out your first loan. The answer depends somewhat on the payment plan that you set up with the insurance company. If you paid an annual premium up front, you should be able to take a loan out almost immediately within the limits of the cash value. If you pay premiums monthly, quarterly, or semiannually, you may have to check with your insurance company to see what your options are for how soon you can take out a loan.

If you are paying more into your policy than just the basic policy amount (and remember I recommended this if you are trying to grow cash value faster and increase the efficiency of your policy), get your agent to explain how you can make an annual premium payment for the basic policy amount, and then set up a monthly amount going into your LPUAR. Let's say your basic Life insurance premium was $2,400 a year for basic Life Insurance coverage, but you want to pay total premiums into your policy of $5,000 a year. You pay an annual premium of $2,400 once a year, and then set up monthly payments of $216.66 a month going into LPUAR. The agent will give you specific limits on the minimum and maximum you can pay into your LPUAR. This gives you flexibility through the year to almost stop monthly payments going in, or increase payments if you get a raise or come into other money.

The steps illustrated in this chapter are straightforward and to the point. To quote Vector in Despicable Me, "Go by the name of Vector. It's a mathematical term, a quantity represented by an arrow with both direction and magnitude." Hopefully, at this point, you are feeling like Vector with laser-like focus and enthusiasm to get your financial life on the straight and narrow.

Chapter 9:

Resources

"Most people have no idea of the giant capacity we can immediately command when we focus all of our resources on mastering a single area of our lives."

- Tony Robbins

This chapter is devoted to getting you resources to make sure you can properly put a solid plan in place. Some of the information is more general in nature, and some is more specific. I cannot possibly list the universe of available sources, but I will try to get you pointed in the right direction. I will list the resources in the order they were presented in the book.

Setting Goals:

It is good to dream big. I do believe that you should have an open mind and list all of your dreams when you are initially planning your retirement. However, it is also wise to be realistic about the goals you are listing. Saving more and saving earlier is still very good advice, but it also needs to be realistic and true to your own situation. More realistic retirement planning will seek to offer the best and most creative approaches to the vexing problems people face without presuming that they have been irresponsible just because their planning is not yet as advanced as they might like it to be.

Quantifying goals:

Once you have listed your goals, you will want to quantify them. To properly quantify cost into the future, you, or the agent you are working with, should factor inflation into the projection. If we have a cost of $ 2,000 today, the cost would be $ 3,257.79 assuming 5 % inflation and 10 years of compounding. The online calculator referenced in the link below will allow you to put in the present value or cost of something today, and based on an interest or inflation rate, it will project what those future values or cost will be worth X years later.

http://tcalc.timevalue.com/all-financial-calculators/investment-calculators/future-value-calculator.aspx

Figuring out your nest egg:

There are many retirement calculators available on the internet. I like the one below because it allows you to see how your money works over time, as well as providing an analysis through retirement. The link is:

http://www.calcxml.com/calculators/retirement-calculator

Kiplinger has a nice calculator as well. The link is:

http://www.kiplinger.com/tool/retirement/T047-S001-retirement-savings-calculator-how-much-money-do-i/index.php

Choosing a company to work with:

This is not an easy question, so you should do your own research on it. I am no longer affiliated with any financial companies, and as I mentioned in the front of the book, I am not trying to specifically steer you toward any particular company. If you want to design the type of policy that I mentioned in the book, then you want to stick with a strong financial company, a mutual company, preferably non direct recognition company, participating policy with good dividends, and you want a level paid up additions rider (LPUAR). I can point you in several directions, but the choice is yours. I will list some resources, and you can decide which way you want to go:

To get a list of great mutual life insurance companies, you can google "Great Life Insurance Companies" or "Top Mutual Insurance Companies".

As of the time of this publication, June 2013, the following companies are non direct recognition companies:

Lafayette Life
Massmutual
Met Life
New York Life
Ohio National

You could reach one of these companies directly. You could also ask an agent that you already know if they sell policies from any of these companies.

However, there is also a way to go directly to a website that puts you in touch with a financial advisor that is already familiar with the strategies mentioned in this book. Take a look at the website below:

http://www.bankonyourself.com/

This is a website written by Pamela Yellen. You will see a button on the right hand side that says "**Request your free Analysis**". You can click this button, fill out some initial information, and it will put you in touch with an advisor that is familiar with the strategies mentioned in this book.

Books to read to get more information on Whole Life Insurance:

There is a book by Pamela Yellen titled <u>Bank on Yourself</u>. I strongly recommend you read it as it has some in depth explanations of the concepts mentioned in this book, as well as stories and testimonials of people who have successfully applied the concepts.

<u>Becoming Your Own Banker</u>, by R. Nelson Nash, is another excellent book that explains the intricacies of a Whole Life policy and an introduction to what is called Infinite Banking. It explains the power of dividend paying whole life insurance.

Ideas related to what we have been talking about.

The following websites and books are recommended if you want to further understand some of the concepts mentioned in this book (type in exact web address listed below):

http://www.wealthconscious.com/?hop=want2plan

http://www.asaferetirement.net/offer/your-safe-retirement-package/?hop=want2plan

http://www.briankim.net/discount/hiddensecret.php?hop=want2pl an

http://www.yousaveontaxes.com/ultimate-guide.html?hop=want2plan

http://www.livingonadime.com/e-store/?hop=want2plan

http://powercouponer.com/become-a-power-couponer?hop=want2plan

http://www.federalgrantsource.org/offer/?hop=want2plan

Chapter 10:

Conclusion

"You can lead a horse to water, but you can't make it drink"

- Proverb

Congratulations!!! YOU now know EVERYTHING you need to know to take a simple concept and free up your money today while saving for retirement. You now truly do have information that only the wealthy have known, but having the information alone will not make you wealthy. You have to take action and put this information to use. There is much more to know but you know all the basics. You have enough to get every one of your family members on the path to financial success.

You should never stop learning no matter how much you know. If you want to learn more, be sure to read some of the following books or websites from the following list to round out your education:

Books:

Bank on Yourself, by Pamela Yellen

Becoming Your Own Banker, by R. Nelson Nash.

Other Websites and Books:

http://www.wealthconscious.com/?hop=want2plan

http://www.asaferetirement.net/offer/your-safe-retirement-package/?hop=want2plan

http://www.briankim.net/discount/hiddensecret.php?hop=want2plan

http://www.yousaveontaxes.com/ultimate-guide.html?hop=want2plan

http://www.livingonadime.com/e-store/?hop=want2plan

http://powercouponer.com/become-a-power-couponer?hop=want2plan

http://www.federalgrantsource.org/offer/?hop=want2plan

Any of the above will give you good information.

Take action, follow through with this book; and then laugh at all those know-it-alls when they start talking about the markets.

As a final logic check, ask yourself the following:

Are you going to put money toward retirement?

Will you be paying for major purchases throughout your lifetime?

Do you currently use credit cards or some sort of financing when purchasing CARS, VACATIONS, COLLEGE, PAYING OFF DEBT, EMERGENCIES, etc?

Do you like not having to watch markets and anticipate the perfect asset allocation?

Do you want a defensive strategy in place?

Even if you had answered "no" to some of the above, you may want to remember that spreading your assets around is a good idea. Having a safe haven to get cash, whenever and for whatever, has a strong appeal. Not having to worry about the government, your company, or the markets will allow you to further diversify your holdings and give you some peace of mind. You may want to compliment your current planning with some of the concepts mentioned in the book. Look strongly at your children, for they could be the biggest beneficiaries of some of the information which I have presented in this book.

I recommend reading this book through one more time, then using it as a guide the third time through. You need to make yourself do this. Many people reading this book will have gained the knowledge, but they will say, "I'll start tomorrow". The next day the same thing. And so on and so on. Do not be one of those people!!! Don't let this book be ten dollars you wasted, let this book be ten dollars spent that changed your life financially forever!!

Financial Freedom is now in reach!!

If you are on a deserted island and found this book, or if you are an Amazon prime member and read it for free, borrowed it from a friend, or read it during a free promotion, please show your thanks and pay for this book simply by rating it! I truly appreciate every rating I get! Thank You!

Like us on Facebook at How to Save For Retirement and Use Your Savings TODAY.

I do hope the information in this book can be a benefit to you!

About the Author

Dan Chipman lives in Lynchburg, Virginia, with his wife and daughter. Dan has worked as a Financial Advisor with Morgan Stanley Dean Witter and as an Agent with Northwestern Mutual. He has an MBA from the University of Illinois and a BSME from the University of Virginia. He is currently working as a District Accountant with the State of Virginia. While working as an advisor and agent for many clients, Dan applied traditional planning strategies to assist clients with meeting their financial goals. However, while working as an advisor, he realized that most of the traditional products have limited capabilities and do not do enough to help us realize a retirement that is relatively risk-free, stable, and something we can count on and predict with accuracy. He also realized that saving generally meant living very lean to acquire future wealth. He set up some of his own policies while still in the financial services industry, and some after he got out of the industry. After leaving the financial services industry, he fully pursued how to live better today while setting up a more stable retirement. After realizing that you truly could have your cake and eat it too, and make your savings grow while using it to better your cash flow today, and pay yourself back, he decided to write this book. All of the techniques, practices, and strategies mentioned in this book have been successfully used by Dan Chipman.

General Disclaimer

All information in this book is provided as general in nature with no guarantee of completeness, accuracy, or timeliness. Your use of the information is at your own risk. You assume full responsibility and risk of loss resulting from the use of this information. Daniel Chipman will not be liable for punitive damages or any other damages relating to the use of this information. Daniel Chipman is not engaged in rendering legal, accounting, or other professional services. The services of a competent professional should be sought if accounting, financial, legal, or tax advice is required. Information provided is for illustrative purposes only. New or revised laws, market changes, or other conditions may change after the time of this writing in June, 2013. Therefore, all rates or assumptions used are not guaranteed and may be subject to change. Each person has unique factors for their particular situation, and results may vary.